THE
BIG
BANG
BOOK

By

Asa Stahl

Illustrated By

Carly Allen-Fletcher

And it begins:

Once upon a time,

we don't know.

Maybe it was dark.

Maybe there was nothing.

For a very,

v

e

r

y

long time.

But then we know —

— there was something.

This! ——

At first, the universe was small

(put your finger over it

and it's gone)

But in less than a second, it grew

10,000,000,00 000,000,000,000

,000,000,000,

000,000,000,000

times

And kept **growing**

It was a hot, messy,
churning soup that cooled.

And fell together neatly...

...into beautiful shapes.

We call them **galaxies.**

Each is made up of thousands of millions of stars.

And each star is as big as a billion
of all the Earth's oceans.

Instead of fish, light swims around in them and bursts out into space.

If you look closely at a star, you might see planets huddled around it

like a candle in the dark.

Some planets are huge swirling balls of gas

boiling away from the
heat of their too-close stars.

Others are too far away

and freeze over like snowballs.

At the edge of one galaxy

around one star

there's a planet
that's just right.

And on that planet

is you.

And everyone else.

The story of the universe is our story.

And maybe, in some distant galaxy

or in our very own Milky Way,

on another planet that's just right,

it's someone else's story, too.

backwards in time, we see that the universe gets more and more dense the farther back we go until we hit a time around 14 billion years ago when the universe was so dense that our current understanding of physics is not complete enough for us to definitively interpret it. This epoch, called the singularity, is as far back as we can trace the history of the universe — we don't know what, if anything, came before the singularity. We need to come up with new ideas about physics to answer such questions.

We do know that following the singularity, the universe expanded and cooled quickly, like billowing steam. This initial expansion was the Big Bang.

In one second, the universe grew in scale by a factor of 10^{43}, the huge number on the fourth page of this book.[1] This amount is so big that none of us has a hope of grasping it intuitively. If you took a penny and blew it up to be the size of the Sun, and then took that gigantic penny and blew it up again the same amount — three more times — you would come close to this factor by which the universe grew in just the first second after the singularity.

In our story of the universe, we described the era that followed as "a hot, messy, churning soup." This phrase is the only part of *The Big Bang Book* inconsistent with current science — all because of the word soup. In a soup or any other liquid, most electrons are bound to protons through the electromagnetic force because opposites attract. But when the universe was young, it was so hot that electrons were careening around too fast for most to be captured by protons. Instead, they moved around freely. This is called a plasma — but it was still very hot and messy. In fact, the universe had to cool for over 400,000 years before electrons began binding to protons, making hydrogen gas. Most of the matter we see in space is in this form, from twinkling stars to colorful nebulae.

200 million years later, these clouds of hydrogen gas collapsed to create the very first stars.

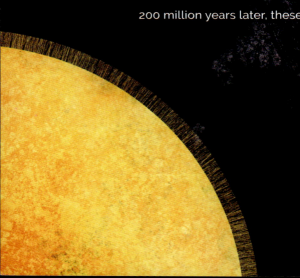

Whenever a star forms, there is some leftover material that orbits around the star in the shape of a disk, like the rings around Saturn. It is in these disks that all planets are born — including our own — but we aren't sure exactly how. The most popular explanation is that tiny grains of dust in the disk collide and stick together like snowflakes, fragile at first, but slowly building up to the size of rocks, then boulders, then huge asteroids, until a planet is born. What remains of the disk then falls into the star, leaving behind the planets and asteroids.

4.5 billion years ago, the Earth, along with seven other planets, formed in a disk around the Sun. But is this story typical for the universe? Do all stars have planets, let alone eight of them? Do one in eight planets have oceans, like Earth does? What about life?

We have only just begun to answer these questions. In 1992, the first discovery of a planet around a star other than the Sun — an exoplanet — gave us an initial glimpse into what other planets are like in the universe. Since then, astronomers have discovered over 4,000 exoplanets. Some are very different from what we would expect based on our own Solar System. There are planets that orbit their stars in mere hours,[2] planets whose atmospheres are boiling off,[3] and planets that have been slung away from their stars into the darkness of space.[4]

We now know that planets are common throughout the universe. Roughly half of stars like the Sun have at least one Earth-sized planet[5] — a fact that is a major first step toward determining how common potentially life-supporting[6] planets are. Over the next few decades, new discoveries will help us answer questions like, "What are other planets made of?" "What are their atmospheres like?" And "How common are oceans?". We may even answer, "Are we the only life in the universe?"

These questions are not just for astronomers to consider. The gaps in our knowledge let wonder into our lives. They allow room for anyone's imagination to come up with exciting theories, and they inspire generations of future scientists and thinkers. While some questions are more technical, like how a star works or what makes the universe expand, the most basic questions are often the most powerful. Questions like "What am I?" and "Where am I?" cut to the heart of how much we understand about the universe.

After all, it takes more than curiosity to ask questions. It takes determination to seek them out, courage to voice them aloud, and both patience and humility to listen to their full, true answers. A good question connects you to the world around you, whether you're wondering why the sky is blue, how lightbulbs work, or how to be a good person.

In writing this more detailed description, a great deal has still been left out. It is the hope of the author that those who read this book will not only gain a better sense of their own world and its origins, but will be able to see the negative spaces in the storytelling, the bits left out, and feel drawn to seek their own answers.

Notes

1: This number was chosen to be representative of the physics involved. Our incomplete under-standing of a process called cosmic inflation prevents it from being definitive.
2: PSR J1719-1438 b
3: GJ 436 b
4: OGLE-2012-BLG-1323
5: Within a 100 day orbit. There may be plenty of others in farther orbits we have yet to detect.
6: Specifically, Earth-like life. We know of no other forms of life, so this is where we begin our search.

Acknowledgments

The author would like to thank Rice University Profs. Christopher Johns-Krull and Mustafa Amin for their support and encouragement in the writing of this book.

References

Bailes, M. et al. 2011, *Science*, vol. 333, pp. 1717-1720
Beust, H. et al. 2014, *Astronomy & Astrophysics*, vol. 561, id. A43
Borucki, W. J. et al. 2012, *Astrophysical Journal*, vol. 745, pp. 120-136
Borucki, W. J. et al. 2013, *Science*, vol. 340, pp. 587-590
Ehrenreich, D. et al. 2015, *Nature*, vol. 522, pp. 459-461
Encrenaz, T. (2004). *The solar system (3rd ed.)*. Berlin: Springer. pp. 89
Fulton, B. J. et al. 2017, *Astronomical Journal*, vol. 154, pp. 109-128
Gillon, M. et al. 2016, *Nature*, vol. 533, pp. 221-224
Jenkins, J. M. et al. 2015, *Astronomical Journal*, vol. 150, pp. 56-75
Mayor, M., Queloz, D. 1995, *Nature*, vol. 378, pp. 355-359
Mroz, P. et al. 2017, *Nature*, vol. 548, pp. 183-186
OGLE Collaboration et al. 2019, *Astronomy & Astrophysics*, vol. 622, pp. 201-209
Owen, J. E., Wu, Y. 2017, *Astrophysical Journal*, vol. 847, pp. 29-43
Rice, Patricia C., Moloney, Norah 2016. *Biological Anthropology and Prehistory: Exploring Our Human Ancestry*. Routledge. pp. 636
Rowe, J. F. et al. 2014, *Astrophysical Journal*, vol. 784, pp. 45-65
Schlebusch, C. M. et al. 2017, *Science*, vol. 358, no. 6363, pp. 652-655
Sumi, T. et al. 2011, *Nature*, vol. 473, pp. 349-352
Winn, J. N. 2018, *Planet Occurrence: Doppler and Transit Surveys, Handbook of Exoplanets*, pp. 195-213

This publication has made use of the NASA Exoplanet Archive, which is operated by the California Institute of Technology, under contract with the National Aeronautics and Space Administration under the Exoplanet Exploration Program.